HOMOEOPATHIC ARROWS -2

CORE AND SOUL OF THE REMEDY (PART -2)

DR. SANDEEP SAIRAL

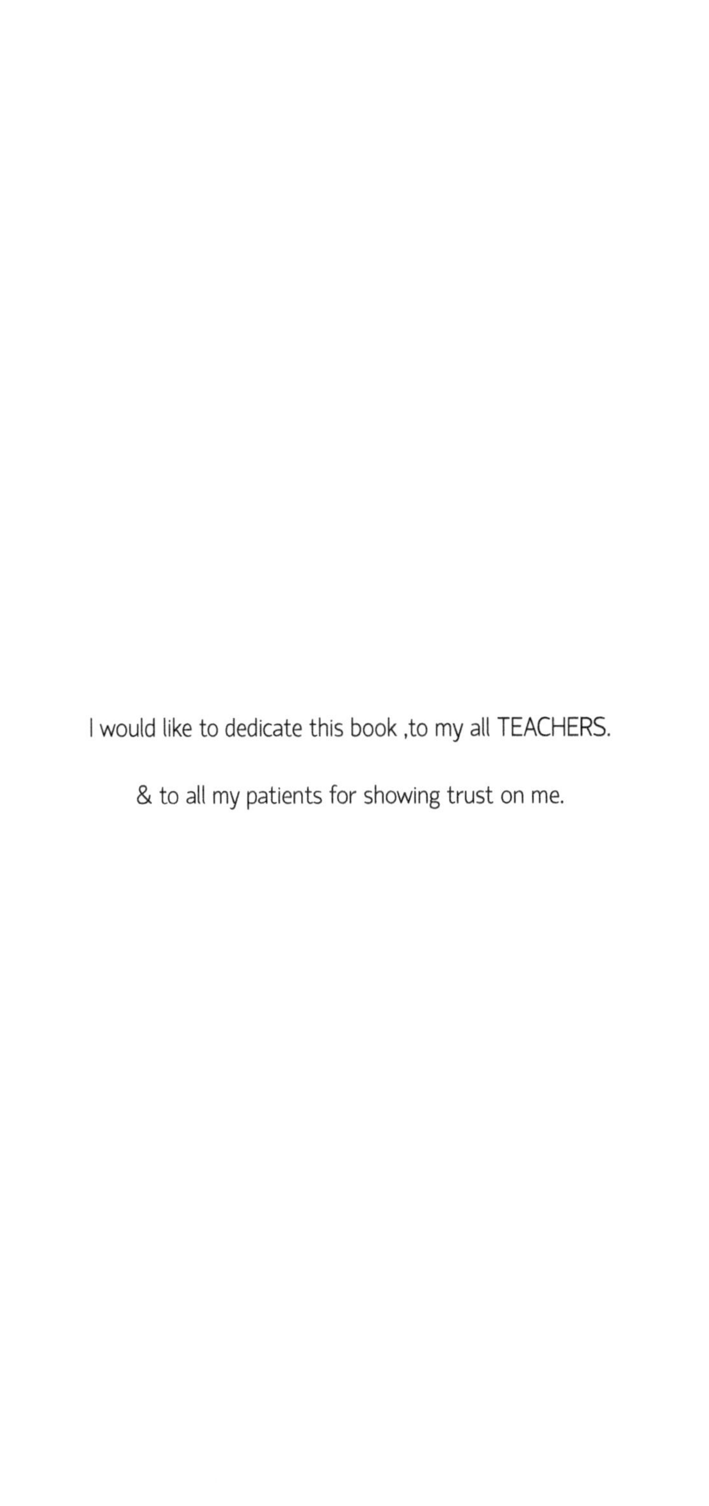

I would like to dedicate this book ,to my all TEACHERS.

& to all my patients for showing trust on me.

Contents

Contents

Foreword

FOREWARD

HOMOEOPATHIC ARROWS -2

3"D"

CORE & SOUL OF THE REMEDY (PART-2)

- As this book is focusing on mental generals of **SICK &** **REMEDY.**

- In mental generals we need to know:-
- Will/ **DESIRES**
- Hates/ **AVERSIONS**
- Loves/ **CARVING**
- Emotions
- Anger, grief, fear, perversion, sensitivity, greed, **GUILT, REGRET,** jealousy, anticipation, suspicion, obstinacy, depression, impulsive, impatience, indifference, speed, reactions (slowness/ hasty), laughing/ weeping, loquacity/ non communicative, consolation.
- Intellect- Memory, concentration, mistakes.
- Understanding- **EASY/ DIFFICULT,** delusion, illusion, hallucination, delirium.

And whatever enter, *DEEP IN THE MIND.*

*REACHES*the *SUBCONSCIOUS LEVEL OF MIND*

All are reflected in the form of **DREAMS.**

DR. SANDEEP SAIRAL
B.H.M.S (DELHI)

Preface

HOMOEOPATHICARROWS

(PART- II)

What applied to **(PART-I)** applied to **(PART-II)**also.

In **PART-I OF HOMOEOPATHIC ARROWS,**as I mentioned about-

"HYPOTHALAMUS- PITUITARY- ADRENAL AXIS."

It justify-

1} The **INFINITESIMAL**(small)**DOSE**of homeopathic medicine is enough (just like hormones).

2} It also answer how such a infinitesimal (small).

Dose of homoeopathic medicine choose its *SPHERE OF ACTION*so easily (as hypothalamus govern whole neuro- endocrine) and has its own axis (examples)-

[**A.**Hypothalamus- Pituitary- Gonadal- Axis]

[**B.**Hypothalamus- Pituitary- Adrenal- Axis]

[**C.**Hypothalamus- Pituitary- Thyroid- Axis]

[**D.**Hypothalamus- Posterior- Pituitary]

3}It also justify when a homoeopath say that [x]medicine act better in day time or to be **GIVEN IN DAY TIME**and[Y]medicine act in different time suppose at night or to be **GIVEN IN NIGHT.**

(As hormones flow or follow *circadian cycle*).

Above all, I will say never to have **RIGID/FIXED IDEAS** about anything. Always follow & believe in **SCIENTIFIC PROCEDURE OF OBSERVATION**

DR. SANDEEP SAIRAL

B.H.M.S. (DELHI)

PREFACE for

HOMOEOPATHIC ARROWS (PART - 1)

The intention to write this book is to make homoeopathic prescription more *sure* and *confident*.

During case taking we note down the changes in physical and mental generals. We mainly cover (appetite, thirst, temperature, stool , urine, perspiration, sexual drive , fear, behaviour etc).

Actually these all changes are induced by,

Hypothalamus – pituitary – adrenal axis.

(as a secondary reaction to illness)

these changes are considered by Homeopathic Physicians as an indication for the *selection of their remedy*.

{ **HYPOTHALAMUS**(maintains the *body's internal balance*,it is body's *natural homeostatic area*)}

Dr. Kent says – " it is a waste of time to run out all the little symptoms if the remedy has the generals."

Dr. Kent and his followers says-

" SYMPTOMS OF THE MIND ARE THE MOST IMPORTANT SYMPTOMS IN THE REMEDY AND IN THE SICK."

Dr. Kent says " *the* **loves and hates or desires and aversions** are the *deepest* mental symptoms"

According to my observation and experience I have noticed that **Dreads ,Dreams , and Desires** 3 "D" are all interconnected.

Dreams, Dreads, and Desires (**3 "D"**) Give *insight into the* remedy and sick. While selecting the remedy if we somehow cover these aspects (**3 "D"**) . We can make a *solid and unshakeable prescription.*

These three DREAMS, DREADS AND DESIRES (**3"D"**) cover *core and soul of the remedy.*

DR. SANDEEP SAIRAL

B.H.M.S.(delhi)

Acknowledgements

I would like to thanks all my patients ,for showing trust on me.

My family for supporting me always, especially my **MOTHER.**

Thanks .

Dr Sandeep Sairal.

Prologue

MATERIA MEDICA

CONTENT

26.   CONCLUSION

CHAPTER ONE

ALLIUM CEPA

ALLIUM CEPA

(RED ONION)
  (HOT & THIRSTY)
  LEFT SIDED (2+)
  LEFT to RIGHT (1+)
  FAST PULSE (1=)
  They have many **DREAMS** –
Dream Of **high waves** (mean situations beyond our control),

DREAM of **CLIFF** (means no way forward or backward),

DREAM of **FALLING INTO WELL** (means you are in great trouble and need help to get out of it, or means you are not emotionally ok),

DREAM of **SEA STORM** (means you are at centre of mental or emotional turmoil),

DREAM of **DEEP WELL** (means depth of your emotions),

DREAM of rapid transit from place to place, DREAM of battles, anger, high place, frightful, fight.

They are dissatisfied, having restless mind. They have difficulty in concentration, **SLUGGISH** and dullness. They are often very anxious with catarrh. **FEAR** that pain will become unbearable. They become melancholic. Mostly absent minded or confused especially after COFFEE AND WINE.

Their nose is SENSITIVE to unpleasant odour especially of **FLOWER OR PEACHES**. So they usually have coryza from odour of **peaches or flowers**.

Coryza especially from **LEFT NOSTRIL(allium cepa give instant & strong relief in many patients for this.)**

< SPRING, AUTUMN, AUGUST, SALAD, CHANGE OF WEATHER.

They have **DESIRE** of rubbing eyes, **DESIRE** of *raw onion* and vegetables.

CHAPTER TWO

AMMONIUM CARBONICUM

AMMONIUM CARBONICUM

(CHILLY & THIRSTY/ THIRSTLESS)
  RIGHT SIDED (2+)
  RIGHT to LEFT (1+)
  SYCOSIS (1+)

This is deep acting, an anti- psoric, constitutional medicine.

They have **AVERSION** to answer, to opposite sex, water (children dislike washing), *GOING OUT,* motion, *BATHING*, milk, meat, open air.

< Other's talk, talking, conversation, thinking, mental exertion, uncovering, waking, *WET,CLOUDY, RAW WEATHER,* potatoes, sweet, hot food and drink.

They **DESIRE** to be silent, travel, cold drink, sweet, sugar, sour.

>Long after eating, dry weather.

They have **FEAR/DREAD** of apprehension, death, of evil, *DISEASES,* misfortune, *BATHING,* on waking.

They are *SPINELESS,*(weakness of will), vindictive, slander disposition, *QUARRELSOME ESPECIALLY DURING MENSES,* unsympathetic, discontented, disobedience, they attempts to escape from their children, family, inadvertence *NEVER LAUGHING, NEVER SUCCEEDS,* spoiled and obstinate children.

There is prostration of mind from mental exhaustion . They have active mind but soon get exhausted.

They are extravagance and *IMMORAL, UNTRUSTWORTHY, UNCLEANLINESS.* They have **DREAMS** of *LICE* (means you need to be careful that others don't fool you).

DREAM of **VERMIN** (means someone near you, don't have good intention).

DREAM of **DISEASE** (means negativity, sorrow, despair).

DREAM of **JOURNEY** (means you have to discipline your life and habits).

DREAM of **DOGS** (means loyalty, trust or means you are deprived of kind and faithful friend in life).

DREAM of *HUMILIATION, HORSES,* ghosts, long past events, death, dead bodies, danger, animals, *SHAMEFUL, ROMANTIC,* recalling things long forgotten.

They readily catch cold in winter.

" **STOPPAGE OF NOSE, AT NIGHT,** with long continued coryza, must breath through mouth."

So they wakes up with suffocative feeling and *feels sleepiness during day time.*

CHAPTER THREE

ANTIMONIUM CRUDUM

ANTIMONIUM CRUDUM

(HOT/CHILLY & THIRSTLESS)
    LEFT SIDED (2+)
    PSORA (2+)
    SYCOSIS (1+)
    FAST PULSE (1+)
    SLOW PULSE (1+)

Disagreeable events and tormenting thoughts about the past, make their life loathing and disgusting. They are always absorbed and buried in their thoughts.

Whatever is done fails to give them satisfaction. They ***WALK WITH DOWNCAST EYES*** to evade look of others.

They become ***RUDIMENTARY/ UNREFINED*** both mentally and physically. Rude/ obstinate/ naughty children. They eat beyond their capacity (over consumption like rudimentary people) and do ***CONSTANT BELCHING*** leads to,

" THICK, MILKY WHITE COATING ON TONGUE."

They have many **DREAMS –**

DREAM of *ACCIDENT*(means *crashing of hopes*).

DREAM of *WOUND-* (means *grief, anger, distress, failure*).

DREAM of *FEASTING* – (means *eating and drinking*).

DREAM of *SOLEMNITIES* – (means *serious and dignified*).

DREAM of *MISFORTUNE, EXHAUSTION.*

DREAM of *DISEASE* – (mean negativity).

DREAM of *BEING WOUNDED* – (means *emotional wound*)

DREAM of *SOMEONE CALLING OUT* – (means reminding of yours strength and weakness).

DREAM of **OLDSCHOOLMATE** – (mean you *want to have more fun* in your waking life),

DREAM of injuries, quarrels, old friends, friends.

These all **DREAMS** are actually representation of **THEIR DESIRES/DREADS**

They have **FEAR/DREAD** of evil, misfortune, death, noise and touch.

AVERSION for – everything, company, being touched, *BATHING,* motion, mother's milk.

< From- company ,presence of other ,cannot bear to be looked at ,*UNCOVERING,WASHING,COLD BATHING, OVEREATING,* sour fruit, pan cake, pastry, strawberries, change of weather.

>Open air, cold application, warm bathing, fasting, epistaxis.

They have DESIRE for *ideal women*, to be carried, to remain in bed, to be silent, *PICKLE,* RAW FOOD, *CUCUMBER, PICKLED MEAT*, spices (highly seasoned food), sour.

CHAPTER FOUR

ANTIMONIUM TARTARICUM

ANTIMONIUM TARTARICUM

TARTAR EMETIC
   (THIRSTLESS)
   LEFT SIDED (2+)
   PSORA (1+)
   SYCOSIS (1+)

They have **FEAR** of **SUFFOCATION**, death, disease, he will not recover, touch, of being alone.

They clings to attendants, melancholic, and complaints of numerous suffering with despair/ doubt of their recovery,nothing can be done to please them.

" When the patients cough there appears to be a large collection of mucous in the bronchi *IT SEEMS AS IF MUCH WOULD BE EXPECTORATED, BUT NOTHING COMES UP.*"

See, most of their COUGH AND DYSPNOGA *BETTER BY SIMPLY ERUCTATION.*

>Open air, **eructation**, flatus, bathing, fanned, vomiting, walking fast, cold food and drink."Even their nausea get

BETTER BY SIMPLE ERUCTATION."

But they get easily frighten, discouraged and biting their nails. Their mood keeps on alternating, anger with cheerfulness.

They have ***AVERSION*** to solitude, touched, mother's milk, ***APPLE.***

They have **DESIRE** to bite, to be carried, company, fruit, juicy things, butter milk, ***APPLE,*** cold drink. They have sensitivity toward **APPLE,** (*either* **DESIRE,***aggravation or aversion for APPLEin any phase of life*).

< ***APPLE,*** fruit, spring, autumn, change of weather, over eating, presence of others, presence of strangers, weeping.

COUGH < CRYING

They have **DREAM** of previous events, exhausting, joyous, difficulties,

DANGER FROM FIRE, FIRE (*means you are* **HEADING INTO DANGER & NEED TO BE CAUTIOUS**)

DREAMof ***WADING IN WATER*** (*means you are able to take control of your feelings*),

DREAMof ***PREACHING*** (*means you* **feeling guilty** *of something you have done consciously or unconsciously wrong*).

CHAPTER FIVE

APIS MELLIFICA

APIS MELLIFICA

(THE HONEY BEE)
(HOT & THIRSTLESS)
LEFT SIDED (2+)
RIGHT SIDED (3+)
RIGHT to LEFT (2+)
PSORA (1+)
They have variable mood. They undertakes many things but preserves in nothing. They keep on POSTPONING EVERYTHING TO NEXT DAY. From mental exhaustion, there is prostration of mind. They become discontented with everything. They get offended easily, they take everything in bad part. They have **AVERSION** to jesting/ JOKES/ HUMOR. They are hard to please, nothing seems to satisfy them. They develop disposition to contradict everything . they are better when occupied, diverted (so they keep themselves fruitlessly busy).

>Undressing, uncovering, open air, cold bathing, cold water, cold application, after stool (diarrhoea), fanned, eating.

They have **AVERSION** to solitude, food, water and drink.

They **DESIRE** to rub eyes, to *wash face in cold water*, fanned, cold air (so must have windows open), uncovering, company, to break things, cold bathing, cold drink, cold milk.

They have **DREAD/FEAR** OF- Death ,of being alone (they cannot bear to be left alone), heart disease, sharp pointed things, of pins, of being poisoned, of suffocation, of touch.

< Hot weather, stove, warm wrap, warm room, warm bed, summer season, spring season, hot drink, *WALKINGFAST,* pickle.

They have **DREAMS, DREAMS** of quarrels, hot stove, assembled people, *jumping greatleaps*, disease, diarrhoea,

flying (means freedom),

physical exertion, full of invention, frightful, **being a girl**, painful body parts,

dirty roads, walking on dirty road (means *moody personality* or **DESIRE** to escape from their daily life RESPONSIBILITIES).

DREAM of *walking over hot floor*.

"HOT PALMS"

CHAPTER SIX

ARUM TRIPHYLLUM

ARUM- TRIPHYLLUM

(INDIAN TURNIP)

LEFT SIDED (1+)

" NOSE FEELS STOPPED IN SPITE OF WATERY DISCHARGE. "

There is IRRITATION causing inflammation of mucous membrane and destruction of tissue.

There is *SHARPNESS, HARSHNESS, CORROSIVENSS, IRRITATION,* which make them restless, excessively cross and obstinate, stubborn, irritability and absent mindedness.

They keep on bitting nail, picks at bed clothes, trying to grasp or reach at *NOSE, LIPS.* Picking nose or lips until it bleeds.

They have coryza from *LEFT NOSTRIL* and discharge from nose is excoriating, ichorous. Even you find they have *OBSTRUCTION OF ESPECIALLY LEFT NOSTRIL.*

They have **DESIRE** to BITE fingers, or BITE himself, to cold drink.

DREAMS - NIGHTMARES.

HOARSENESS in public speaker and singer. From over use of voice.

" DESQUAMATION IN LARGE FLAKES ."

CHAPTER SEVEN

BARYTA CARBONICA

BARYTA CARBONICA

(CHILLY & THIRSTY)
   RIGHT to LEFT SIDED (1+)
   PSORA (2+)
   SYCOSIS (2+)
   FAST PULSE (1+)
I have given this remedy more to senior citizens/ old age people rather than children for (***COUGH, COPIOUS-EXPECTORATION,*** *ASTHMATIC/ DIFFICULT RESPIRATION,VERTIGO, FREQUENT URINATION,SLEEPLESSNESS*).

The ***SECOND CHILDHOOD**/* senior citizens.

They are ***SPINELESS, SLOWNESS,***irresolute, yielding, timid or for children with ***SUSPENDED GROWTH.*** Child don't reach upto men or women stage/adult phase.

They have ***SLOW GRASPING POWER*** and have thoughtless behaviour.

They think all visitors laugh at them.

They feel people mocking at them.

They are suspicious that people are talking about them.

They give too lengthy/ expansive demonstration/ communication.

They have lack of confidence and suffer from *INFERIORITY COMPLEX* from the very beginning of their life.

They avoid social gathering and society just *STICK CLOSE TO THEIR OWN FAMILY.*

They have tendency to take cold and everytime their tonsils get swollen

"THEY GET TIRED, EVEN WHILE EATING"-many patients says this.

They have **FEAR/DREAD** of*STRANGERS,* of people, children, of *GOING BY RAIL,*of others approaching him, crossing a bridge, in crowd, of public place, from noise in street, something bad will happen.

They are pessimist and narrow minded, neglect everything.

< Presence of *STRANGER, COMPANY,* thinking of complaints, fasting, physical exertion.

They have *AVERSION* to *COMPANY,* laughing, to play in children, reading , mental work, bathing, fruit, *PLUMS.*

They have **DESIRE** to hide, (*especially from STRANGERS*), magnetized, nibble, to be silent, to travel, warm clothing.

>Magnetized, occupied/ diverted, long after eating or during eating, perspiration.

They have **DREAM** of dead bodies, confused,

DREAM of adventure (*means **your boring and routine life**).*

DREAM of *DISEASE(means, unpleasantness, negativity, sorrow and despair).*

DREAM of *FIRE(means you are heading into danger, you need to be cautious).*

DREAM of *SORE THROAT(means difficult communication).*

DREAM of *QUARREL, MISFORTUNE.*

"BITTING NAILS & OFFENSIVE FOOT SWEAT".

CHAPTER EIGHT

BELLADONNA

BELLADONNA

DEADLY NIGHTSHADE
   (CHILLY + THIRSTY/THIRSTLESS)
   RIGHT SIDED (3+)
   RIGHT to LEFT SIDED (1+)
   FAST PULSE (3+)
   SLOW PULSE (2+)

I have recently seen a Bollywood movie **GHAJINI**, the lead actor in this movie remind me of **BELLADONNA (BELL)**.

Person who are lively and entertaining when well, but become violent and devil when sick.

According to me **BELLADONNA** core is **WILDNESS/ WILD OX.**

Complaints appear suddenly and cease suddenly. Ferocious, monstrous, violent and excitable. They have mania of **TEARING, SCRATCHING, BITTING AND STRIKING.** They strike themselves or head against wall. They strike on their **FACE** and **ABDOMEN.** Throw things at other person. They tear things, they tear their **HAIR, NIGHT DRESS, BEDCLOTHES** and **THEMSELVES.** They simply have impulse to do strange things or to behave in **UNREASONABLE** or **UNACCEPTABLE** way, **QUARRELSOME, SELF TORTORE** or they **TORMENT** themselves. They love to make people and animals suffer *(CRUELTY)*. They are **EAGER/ QUICK** to **ARGUE, QUARREL, FIGHT.** Most of time they will talk about **BATTLES** and *WARS.*

When well, they are full of kindness, they are cheerful. They **LAUGH, SING, DANCE** and **WHISTLE.**

They have **DREADS/FEARS** of *PARALSIS, OF WATER, OF BEING ALONE ,if left alone they may DIE, OFBEING POISONED, SNAKES, ROBBERS, OF TOUCH, OF BEING STRUCK ,OF TUNNEL, OFSOMETHING UNDER THE BED, OF DOGS, OF GHOSTS, OF DARK, OF CROWD, OF SOLITUDE,Of BODY WILL PUTREFY.*

But when **SICK** or in **VIOLENT/WILD** phase they are **FEARLESS.**

They **DESIRE** To *SPITTING IN PEOPLE's FACES ,TO PULL ONE'S HAIR, TO PULL ONE'STEETH TO KILL, TO BE KILLED, TO BITE THOSE AROUND HIM, TO BITE OBJECT, TO BITE SPOON ,TO BE CARRIED FAST, TO EXCERCISE, TO TRAVEL, TO GO HOME, COMPANY ,TO PLAYHIDE AND SEEK, TO COVER, COLD FOOD AND DRINKS, SOUR, LEMONADE, COFFEE INDIGESTABLE, LIQUID FOOD.*

They have lot of **DREAMS.**

DREAMS:- DANGER OF FIRE,**FIRE** (mean you are heading into danger and need to be cautious).

DREAM of **BEING SHOT** (means inner fear towards-conflicts, arguments and confrontations within your family, friends, colleague and partner).

DREAM of **GYMNSTICS** (Means having difficulties in life and you are trying to overcome them by leap and twist anyhow).

DREAM of **BEING PURSUED BY GAINTS** (means you don't feel comfortable in a work PLACE/situation).

DREAM of **ROBBERS** (means you are feeling powerless).

DREAM of **SHOOTING** (means you need to take some time off from your routine busy life).

DREAM of **ACCIDENTS** (means crashing of your hopes).

DREAM of **GIANTS** (means obstacle and challenges in life).

DREAM OF **VERMIN** (means someone near you does not have good intentions).

DREAM of **FLYING** (means freedom).

DREAM of **FALLING** (means you need to relax, from hidden insecurities, social anxieties or unstable situations in life).

DREAM of **URINATING** (means you need to get rid of the toxins from your life).

DREAM of **BATTLE** (means *you genuinely wish to vent your rage by picking a fight*).

DREAM of **WALKING,**

DREAM of **WATER** (means emotions).

DREAM of **SWIMMING IN WATER** (means you need to cleanse or deal with your emotional issues).

DREAM of *QUARREL, RUNNING, RIDING in aCARRIAGE, MURDER, ASSASSINS,HOUSEHOLD, GHOSTS, ANIMALS, DANGER of DEATH, DIFFICULTIES, EXHAUSTING* and BEING busy.

They have **AVERSIONS** to answer, to presence of others, of even intimate friends, conversation, coffee, eggs, vegetables, soup, *smell of milk.*

< Admonition, warning, reprimand, consolation, **COMBING.** Mental exertion, laughing, cold bathing, washing, coffee, fish, ice, shell fish, sugar, vinegar.

>Cover, after sleep, lemonade

Nausea > Flatus.

Wildness/ State of excitability >**BY EATING LITTLE FOOD.**

Their mood is variable, they are industrious, independent, interesting, cheerful, full of energy, extravagance, impelled to touch everything, taste everything, hasty in eating, drinking and movements. But they get offended easily. Takes everything in bad part. They want to be naked, roving about aimlessly, walks in circle. Restlessly wanders about they live in their own world.

They have delusions of wolves, of wealth, of BEING AT WAR, voice of dead people. Of travelling ,someone is pulling out his tongue, surrounded by friends, snake in and around them, of **RIDING OX**, of pursued by soilders, or by police, by enemies.

They have delirium of urinating outside pot.

"HEAT, REDDNESS, THROBBING AND BURNING WHEREVER IS THE COMPLAINTS."

CHAPTER NINE

BRYONIA

BRYONIA

(WILD HOPE)
  (HOT & THIRSTY)
  RIGHT SIDED (3+)
  LEFT SIDED (2+)
  RIGHT to LEFT SIDED (1+)
  PSORA (1+)
  SYCOSIS (1+)
  FAST PULSE (3+)

I relate this remedy to **SMALL SHOPKEEPERS** and **SOLDIERS** who **WORK UNDERCONSTANT SUNLIGHT exposure.** There is lot of **IRRITABILITY** and **ANGER** inside and **LONLINESS.**

They talk of either business or going home.

They are considered ungrateful due to *AVARICE,* insecurity, materialistic mind.

They are determined, robust, with firm muscular fibre, dark complexion *(under constant sunlight exposure),* with tendency to leanness irritability *(nervous **dry**).*

Their all mucous membranes are **DRY,**

Stool is **DRY,** cough is **DRY,** lips and tongue are **DRY.**

There is dirtiness in everything.

They are industrious and having **AVERSION** to be disturbed. They get irritable when questioned. Contradiction is intolerable to them. They remain discontented with themselves. Feels unfortunate.

They have **AVERSION** to presence of others, company, being disturbed, thinking, being touched, noise, coffee, cabbage, hard boiled eggs, tobacco, smoking.

< Presence of strangers, thinking of complaints.

They have **FEAR** of suffering, starving, poverty, of suffocation, of being alone, of thunder storm.

They have **DESIRE** for change, company, full of **DESIRE**, more than they needs, or things not present, unattainable things, to be held/hold, to go home, to leave home *(change)*, travel, wander, change of position, rest, indigestible, coffee, liquid food, warm soup.

They think a lot about their financial well being.

They are sluggish and non excitable. They *ALWAYS DOMINATE OR WIN IN BARGAINING.*

They have **DREAM** of *anger, physical and mental exertion, excelling in mental work , previous events, dead, dead bodies, business of the day, pain.,*

DREAMof **battle** *(means ability to overcome difficulties).*

DREAM of **quarrels** *(means too much pressure in work),*

DREAM of fight *(mean you genuinely wish to vent your rage by picking a fight or it indicate suppressed ANGER OR FRUSTATION),*

DREAM of riots *(means FEAR AND ANGER),*

DREAM of household, someone tossing out of the window, disease.

There is **DREAM** and **DELUSION** of being pursued by soldiers *(means- longing to go home).*

They worry/ about business/ work.

CHAPTER TEN

CARBO VEGETABILIS

CARBO VEGETABILIS

(CHILLY & THIRSTY)
  PSORA (2+)
  SYCOSIS (1+)
  FAST PULSE (1+)

They have generosity towards strangers, avarice as regard his family. They have indifference to their family, to everything, to their suffering, to music they love. They have dull senses, timid, sluggish, slow thinking and cowardice, have lack of confidence, they have delusion of being forsaken / abandonment.

Due to mental exhaustion *(there)* is prostration of mind, slowness, irresolution. They get easily frightened, discouraged.

They have **FEAR/DREAD** *of STRANGERS, SUFFOCATION, SOMETHING* bad will happen, ghost, death, dark, accident, *OF EATING* or *AFTER EATING.*

They have **DREAM** *of FIRE(means you are heading into danger and need to be cautious).*

DREAM *ofROBBERS(means you are probably feeling powerless),*

DREAM *of WATER* (*means emotions),*
ghosts, frightful, restless, vivid.
>ERUCTATION, LOOSING CLOTHING, FANNED.

< Strangers, mental exertion, company, darkness, laughing, cold air, hot bathing, over eating, perspiration, cabbage, ***BEANS, PEAS, FARINACEOUS FOOD, FLATULENT FOOD***, fish, ice, pickled meat, milk, onion, sauerkraut, vinegar, ***THOUGHT OF FOOD.***

They have **AVERSION** for- ***THINKING,MENTAL WORK,*** company, meat, bathing, cabbage, fish, pickled meat, milk, soup.

They have **DESIRE**- To be carried, to bite, death, to be silent, to be ***FANNED,*** must have ***WINDOWS OPEN,*** bathing, ***COLD AIR***, sweet.

CHAPTER ELEVEN

CONIUM MACULATUM

CONIUM MACULATUM

POISON HEMLOCK
   (CHILLY & THIRSTLESS)
   RIGHT SIDED (3+)
   PSORA (1+)
   SYCOSIS (1+)
   SYPHILIS (2+)
   FAST PULSE (3+)
   SLOW PULSE (2+)
Another good remedy **ESPECIALLY FOR SENIOR CITIZENS,** or for them, who have anxiety from prolonged continence *(means **SELF RESTRAINT,** especially with* **REGARD TO SEX)**

There is suppression of menses, urine *(prostate)*, feeling, sexual DESIRES.

BREAST become sore, hard, enlarged and painful before and during menses.

They are **FULL OF WORRIES** and cares, they neglect important thing. They have chronic fatigues from over work. So mental work become impossible for them. There is **SLOWNESS** of mind. They are **UNRELIABLE IN THEIR**

PROMISES. They make useless purchases, extravagance. They waste their money.

They have mania or like to wear their best clothes *ONE OF MY PATIENT* of cervical spondylosis confessed that *HEDESIREOR WISH TO WEAR "NEW CLOTHES".*

DESIRES of conium- to remain in bed, to be quiet, to be silent, business, to be magnetized,

to rub eyes, cabbage, indigestible (*chalk, clay, slate*)

>**Coition**, occupied, diverted, magnetized, fasting.

They have **FEAR** of *MENTAL WORK,* superstition, touch, robbers, death, crowd of others approaching him, of being alone, night, thunder storm.

While walking on the road. They wants to hold somebody.

" **SEXUAL THOUGHTS KEEP TORMENTING THEM.**"

They have **AVERSION** to answer, to friends, family members, reading, MENTAL WORK, touch, noise, uncovering, open air, bathing.

They have **aversion** and sadness to see their children.

< *MENTAL EXERTION,* thinking of complaints, talks of others, *PUNISHMENTS,* excitement, laughing, uncovering, perspiration, *fast walking,* apple.

They have **DREAM** /delusion of being *PURSUED BY ENEMIES(means real life full of stress)*

They have **DREAM** of *DEAD FRIEND(means you wish your friend were around to help you navigate).*

DREAM of *DEATH* of *FRIEND(means negative feeling like fear, jealous, hated- suppressed* with in you)..

DREAM of *HUMILITION, MUTILATION, QUARREL, RIOTS, SHAMEFUL, DANGER, ACCIDENTS.*

CHAPTER TWELVE

HEPAR SULPHURIS

HEPAR SULPHUR

(CHILLY & THIRSTY)
  LEFT SIDED (1+)
  RIGHTSIDED (2+)
  PSORA (2+)
  SYCOSIS (1+)
  SYPHILIS (2+)
  FAST PULSE (1+)
  SLOW PULSE (1+)
They **ACT QUICKLY,WITHOUT THINKING,** unplanned.

They are impatience. They are hasty in eating, drinking and occupation.

It affect nerves making patient **OVER ORHYPE SENSITIVE** to all impression- to cold, to draught of air, to touch, pain, noise, odour. So they are intolerable, to pressure **(touch),** stress, suffering *(pain).*

They are **FEROCIOUS AND AGGRESSIVE,** wants to kill who offend them, want to set thing on fire. They develop rage from pain, vindictive, they have unfeeling , hardhearted, seen never laughing or cheerful. They want to set things or house on fire. They estranged from their family.

They have **AVERION**- to family members, touched, music, mental work, UNCOVERING, bathing, to play in children.

Even slight cause make him intensely angry, quarrelsome , abusive and impulsive. Impulses to do violence and to destroy. Sometimes impulses are without cause so they

DESIRE for change, refreshing things, fruits, lime, slate, clay, mustard, pickle, potatoes, sour, spicy, tea and vineger.

< Over eating, ice, coffee, cheese, sweets, vinegar, tea, autumn, spring, *UNCOVERING,UNDRESSING.*

They have **FEAR** of touch, thunder storm, snakes, *THEY WILL NOT RECOVER,* of feeling being hurt by others, about health of loved ones, *BEING DISFIGURED, DISEASES,* of being alone, in crowd.

They are full of worries/ care when alone. They have anxiety about his family, health of relative. Being *DISCOURAGED FROM PAIN,* they are always dissatisfied with themselves and everything. They are destructive. They are *TALKATIVE AND WOULD NOTLISTEN TO OTHERS.*

>Flatus, hot bathing, sweating, fasting ,long after eating.

They have DREAMS of purulent expectoration, frightful,

hemoptysis (means some suppressed feeling you have in your real life),

diseases (means negativity, sorrows, despair),

FIRE (means you are heading into danger and need to be cautious),

of broken window (it mean stress and anxiety)

DREAM*of HEARING GUNSHOT (mean you are in danger).*

DREAM off*allingfromHIGH PLACE(means feeling out of control).*

DREAM *of SHOOTING (means sense of underachievement).*

DREAM*of DANGER, QUARRELS.*

After knowing even little bit about **DREAM** interpretation. We can cross question the patient. To know more about their Mental Generals.

CHAPTER THIRTEEN

HYOSCYAMUS NIGER

HYOSCYAMUS NIGER

HENBANE
   (CHILLY & THIRSTY)
   PSORA (1+)
   FAST PULSE (2+)
   SLOW PULSE (1+)
You can easily relate this remedy to few of the movie actors/actress or **WHO WANT TO BE CENTRE OF ATTRACTION.**

They are high spirited, vivacious and talkative. They speak each word louder. They even laugh loudly. They make ridiculous gestures. There is tastelessness in dressing. They dress in *STRANGE* way. They have impulse to do **strange** thing, act in *STRANGE* way. There is wildness in behaviour.

They are suspicious that people are talking about them. They appear in public place in a freakish, outlandish, *STRANGE* manner. They have passion to ridicule, or mocking/jesting.

They are cheerful, dancing, laughing, and singing. They are avarice/ materialistic/ money grubbing as regard to their family. But generous toward **STRANGERS** and squandering on themselves.

They spend mostly on dress ,still dress indecently. They become vindictive with rage. There is destructiveness especially for clothes. They want to be naked during drunkenness. Quarrelsome from jealousy.

They are passionate, playful and have overactive mind. They are **OUT OF TOUCH WITHREALITY.**

They keep on roving about naked aimlessly, wander restlessly. They are impelled to touch everything.

They are in **DELUSION,** that they are **BEING WATCHED ALL THE TIME, WIFE IS FAITHLESS,BEING SOLD,** are being **POISONED,** will be murdered, being pursued by police, enemies.

They have **FEAR** of **BEING SOLD,** of **BEING BETRAYED,** of **BEING POISONED,** of water, from noise of rushing water, of being injured, ghost, **ENEMIES, OF EATING,** after eating food, dogs, death, of being alone, being bitten.

They have **DREAMS** of **BATTLES**(*means you wish to vent your rage or you want to express yourself to someone for a very long time*).

DREAM of **WILD ANIMALS**(*means dangerous and destructive urges, untamed or uncivilised aspects of your personality*),

DREAM of **CATS**(*means someone in your life is malicious*),

DREAM of **DOGS**(*means loyalty, trust*),

DREAM of **FRIGHTFUL,**

DREAM of **HISTORIC**(*means wish to live same experience once again*).

They have **AVERSION** to answer, to everything, mental work, drink, alcohol.

They have **DESIRE** to *REMAIN IN BED(NAKED)*, to bite, bite object, bite everyone who disturb them, to climb, break things, wander, hide, travel, to go home, to kill, to kill everyone when they see knife, to strike, spitting in faces of people, to *(clay, chalk, slate)* indigestible.

< *ANIMATION*, company, *EXCITEMENT,MENTAL EXERTION,* laughing, cold drink, drinking, alcohol, uncovering, *WALKING FAST.*

>Urination, fasting, **vomiting**, **perspiration**, coffee.

"**HICOUGH AFTER EATING.**"

"**LAUGHING LOUD FOR NOTHING.**"

CHAPTER FOURTEEN

IODIUM

IODIUM

(HOT & THIRSTY)
   LEFT to RIGHT SIDED (2+)
   PSORA (1+)
   SYPHILIS(2+)
   FAST PULSE (3+)
   SLOW PULSE (1+)

There is **DREAM** of walking in **MUD, MUD,** wading in **MUD.**

DREAM of **SOILING** himself, of **EXCREMENTS,** of walking in **EXCREMENT,**

DREAM of swimming in water *(means it is time to deal with your emotional issues you may be facing).*

DREAM of **DAUGHTER FALLING INTO WATER***(means your emotions are out of control now).*

DREAM of **ACCIDENTS***(means crashing of hopes).*

DREAM of **SOILING** himself with excrement *(means your ideas are soiled)*

DREAM of **UNSUCCESSFUL IN COITION,** amorous, disgusting and falling into water.

Overall **DREAMS** suggest that IODIUM patient are "**HURTING THEMSELVES WITH THEIR OWN MISTAKES.**"

Patients are compelled to keep doing something in order to draw away their impulses, anxiety and energy. Anxiety-driving place to place. They **EAT MORE THAN THEY SHOULD.** They **PURCHASE/ BUY MORE THAN THEY SHOULD.**

Extravagance, even they forget what they purchase, go and leave them. They constantly feel as if they have forgotten something. They are full of energy, talkative, cheerful, impatience. They keep on running about, never sits or sleep at night. They are hasty in walking.

They are better by physical exertion. They have **EXTREME/ INSATIABLE/ GLUTTONOUS** hunger, with progressive emaciation. They have sudden impulse to run and do violence tendency to do some strange things without any cause.

They have super **FAST ASSIMILATION.**

Their **BASAL METABOLIC RATE** is quite high.

They **BURN THEIR CALORIES VERY FAST.**

They represent the condition very similar to **HYPERTHYROIDISM.**

< Presence of others, conversation, fasting, hunger, summer, warm and wet weather.

>**PHYSICAL EXERTION,** occupied/ diverted, deep respiration, open air,**EATING.**

They have **AVERSION** to answer, approach by persons, to family members, to **BEING APPROACHED,** to company, presence of others, **OF INTIMATE FRIENDS,** avoid the sight of people, **PRESENCE OF STRANGERS,** to sit being touched, hat, milk.

They have **DESIRE** to kill, to kill themselves,*(sudden impulse)*, irresistible impulse to kill a women, to be magnetized, silent, travel, cold bathing, cold air, must have window open, alcohol, meat, refreshing things, stimulants, walking *(night)*.

They have **FEAR/ DREAD** of water, of touch, death, **ACCIDENTS,** something bad will happen, of failure, of **GOING TO DOCTOR,** of people, of **MISFORTUNE,** of manual labour or **AFTER MANUAL LABOUR,** imaginary things, of others approaching him.

CHAPTER FIFTEEN

LEDUM PALUSTRE

LEDUM PALUSTRE

MARSH – TEA
 (HOT & THIRSTY)
 PSORA(1+)
 SYPHILIS(2+)
 FAST PULSE (3+)
 CORE word for led pal is "**CROCODILE**"
They have calmness, stillness .They Are content with themselves.

They have **FEAR** of **CROWD**, of men *(anthrop phobia)*.

They have **FEAR** to go to sleep. They feel, if they go to sleep, they will die.

They have anxiety as if **GUILTY OF A CRIME**.

AVERSION – To – **COMPANY,** presence of others, sight of others, friends, cover, hat.

< **COMPANY,** fast walking

>**UNCOVERING**, getting feet wet, cold bathing.

They **DESIRE** for – uncovering, solitude, cold bathing, cold drinks, alcoholic drinks and tobacco, smoking, mental activity.

From passionate and industrious nature they develop mental exhaustion or prostration of mind we can say. They become discontented, have disgust with everything. They get in repulsive mood, **HATRED REVENGE/ VINDICTIVE** attitude. They hate their fellow beings and avoid company.

Their **DREAMS** clearly indicate their mental generals. What they have deep inside their mind.

DREAMS *of CROCODILE(most important)* in **LED PAL***(means enemies are on the look out to harm you and advises you to BEWARE AND BE CAUTIOUS).*

DREAMS of shameful, violence, restless, humiliation, amorous, mental exertion, being busy, remorse *(DEEP REGRET),*

being pursued by wild animals *(means constantly frightened by someone).*

" **PAINFUL & SWOLLEN ANKLES.**"

" **AFFECTED PART IS COLD >BY COLD APPLICATIONS.**"

CHAPTER SIXTEEN

MEDORRHINUM

MEDORRHINUM

(HOT & THIRSTY)
SYCOSIS (3+)

They have **FEAR/ DREAD** of suffocation, superstitions, of losing self control, of misfortune, of not being able to bear any medicine, of heart disease, something bad will happen, of ghost, death, dark, someone is behind them, of being alone at night.

DESIRE for "ICE" indicated me toward this remedy most of the time,

Other **DESIRES** of *MEDORRHIUM* are- to play at night, to pull one's hair, wander, fanned, cold air, *MUST HAVE WINDOWS OPEN, UNCOVERING,* carbonated fizzy drinks, green fruits, ice- cream, juicy things, raw onion, *ORANGES,* potatoes, sour, sweet, salt, warm drink and food, tobacco, smoking, *ICE.*

>*WEEPING, URINATION,* fanned, undressing, uncovering, *DISCHARGES, EVENING TIME,* eating, drinking.

< Reading, writing, thinking of complaints, *MENTAL EXERTION,* washing feet, *COVERING* (intolerable), *SUNRISE TO SUNSET,* sweet

They have **AVERSION** to responsibility, being touched, **MENTAL WORK,** sweet.

They become crazy from impotency of their mind. Mental exertion make them insane. There is mental dullness. They understand questions only after repeating.

Memory is weak for what they have said or for what they are about to say/ write. There is confusion of their own identity. They forget their own name. There is delusion of rats, mice running across the room.

There is restlessness when attempting to study. Restlessly they wander about, runs about in streets at night.

They keep on roving naked aimlessly.

In O.C.D. They bite their nails, Washes their hand, shakes their feet and hands (fidgety).

They are always in haste, they walk rapidly from anxiety. They think everybody moving too slowly.

"BURNING OF HANDS & FEET."

"Swelling & painful stiffness of **ANKLES.**"

This is the powerful and deep acting medicine indicated for chronic ailments.

They have **DREAMS*of*DISEASE***(means unpleasantness, negativity, sorrow, and despair).*

DREAM ofPAIN*(means signal of danger).*

DREAM of **WALKING** *(warning about your health).*

DREAMof **DRINKING** *(means you feel irresponsible or out of control in waking life)*

DREAM of**EXHAUSTING***(means fatigued due to worry and anxiety).*

DREAMof *GHOST, PHYSICAL EXERTION, DEAD, FRIGHTFUL.*

"INABILITY TO KEEP THEIR LEGS STILL WHEN TRYING TO SLEEP."

CHAPTER SEVENTEEN

OPIUM

OPIUM

(HOT & THIRSTY/ THIRSTLESS)
   RIGHT SIDED (1+)
   PSORA (1+)
   FAST PULSE (3+)
   SLOW PULSE (3+)
They are in **SENSE OF DIVINE PEACE.**

They are completely out of touch with reality.

They have sensation of bodily well being, great happiness, too much generous. They are totally indifferent to pain and pleasure. They are unable to understand or appreciate their sufferings.

They wants nothing, says nothing ails them. We can say they are forgetful of their sufferings. They talk to themselves, mostly superstitious. They waste away their time.

They are unreliable in their promises, unsympathetic. They have increased courage, rash and inconsiderable boldness.

They are **INSENSITIVE/ LACK OF SENSIBILITY.**

This leads to **SLUGGISHNESS, INACTIVITY, SLOWNESS & PAINLESSNESS** conditions.

For an example-

They have no sensitivity even when rectum or urinary bladder is full. The message of fullness is unrecognized by nervous system. We can say **INSENSIBILITY OF NERVOUS SYSTEM.**

They **DESIRE-** Nothing , to bite own arms, fingers, hands or themselves, unattainable things, to kill, to rest, to rub eyes, to go home, leaning against anything, lie down, cold drink, sugar, sweets.

They have **AVERSION** to answer, to tobacco smoking.

They **FEAR** from threatening abortion, from *amenorrhoea*, others approaching them, death, diarrhoea, of being murdered, speaking in public, extravagance, they see frightful visions, mice, scorpions etc. **THEY ARE FEARLESS ALSO.** They run about as if in a fright.

Aliment of opium in many cases is from **FEAR/ FRIGHT.**

They have many **DREAMS-**

DREAM of being stabbed, unsuccessful, **skeleton**, quarrels,

falling from high place(MEANS FEELING OUT OF CONTROL SITUATIOS IN LIFE),

journey *(means they **NEED TO DISCIPLINE THEIR HABITS AND LIFE**),*

Horrible grimaces, ghosts, devils, cats, dogs, black forms.

Dragons(means *YOU HAVE BRAVERY, PATIENCE AND STRENGTH).*

All **DREAMS, DESIRES & DREADS** are interconnected and reflecting the theme of the **REMEDY.**

CHAPTER EIGHTEEN

PSORINUM

PSORINUM

(CHILLY & THIRSTY)
PSORA (3+)
SYCOSIS (1+)
CORE OF THIS REMEDY IS "UNCLEANLINESS"
Best way to know this remedy is to start from **DREAMS.**
DREAM of **STOOL/ EXCREMENT** *(means reflection of* **FREEDOM),**

DREAM of being closet/ excrement closet *(means YOU HAVE NEGATIVE EMOTIONS inside and you need to* **LET IT GO or** *It is TIME FOR INNER PEACE, CLEANING AND RENEWAL).*

DREAM of restless, frightful, danger, business, amorous.

Robbers *(means YOU ARE FEELINGPOWERLESS).*

They have **FEAR/ DREAD OF POVERTY (MOSTLY)** ,of misfortune, something bad will happen, business failure, he think he is going to a poor home, fire, alone, disease, cancer, disaster,

of death during heart symptoms, **busy street**, when riding in a carriage, of thunder storm and causeless.

They feel unfortunate, melancholic, torments everyone with their complaints. They are cheerful when constipated. **FULL OF DIRTINESS,** still have mania of washing hands and feet's, EVEN after bath/ wash, they have filthy/foul/ muddy/dirty smelling. Skin **REMAINS DIRTY.**

Though there is no eruption at night. He is driven to despair by the **CONTINUAL ITCHING,** if he throws the covers off them, he becomes chilly, if he covers up then there is ITCHING.

They have **AVERSION** to company, uncovering, **BATHING,** tobacco, smoking.

They **DESIRE-** to remain in bed, to be near fire, death, cold drinks, sour, indigestible and warm clothing.

< **Uncleanliness**, company, presence of others, mental exertion, uncovering, **BATHING,WASHING,** sour fruits, fasting.

>Eating, perspiration, drinking, nose bleed *(epistaxis)*.

"One of my case, of scanty menses (just for one hour) got cured from psorinum".

CHAPTER NINETEEN

SABADILLA

SABADILLA

(CHILLY & THIRSTLESS)
   RIGHT SIDED (2+)
   LEFT to RIGHT SIDED (1+)
   RIGHT to LEFT SIDED (3+)
   PSORA (1+)
   SYCOSIS (1+)
Mostly used for allergic rhinitis.

They have **CAUSELESS FEAR, FEAR** of water, disease, death, especially of ulcer in/ of stomach *(GASTRIC ULCER).*

Their imagination are groundless, nothing is visible, imaginary illness (hypochondriacally). They have illusion of being sick, of some part of body is deformed, of **GASTRIC ULCER,** of swollen scrotum, of enlarged chin.

They have **DESIRE** for rest, to be silent, to *WASH FACE WITH COLD WATER,* **HONEY,** cold milk, warm food, warm drink, sour, sweet and flour.

They have **AVERSION** to answer, to mental work, labour, coffee, **GARLIC, ONION.**

They have **DREAMS** of **EXCELLING IN MENTAL WORK**, being busy, exertion,

falling *(means* **HIDDEN INSECURITY, SOCIAL ANXIETIES,** *unstable situation in life),* amorous, frightful,

OF HELP *(means shyness/ pride keeping you away from asking for help when you need it most),* many restless,

of **DON'T SUCCEED IN BUSINESS***(means humiliation and helplessness and you are stressed).*

They are cheerful and vivacious.

They have anxiety as if committed a crime, **PROSTRATION OF MIND,** LEAD TOconfusion of mind

They aimlessly, senselessly keep roving.

They have indifference to joke/ jesting, toward others, even for work. They are always buried in thoughts, delusion, so remain absent minded. They feel difficulty in concentration.

< Thinking of complaints, consolation.

While meditating, reading, thinking in a chair, they fall asleep.

"VIOLENT SNEEZING + CORYZA + LACHRYMATION."

CHAPTER TWENTY

SPONGIA TOSTA

SPONGIA

(HOT & THIRSTY)
RIGHT to LEFT SIDED (1+)
PSORA (1+)
SLOW PULSE (1+)
They have strong **DESIRE** for **OPEN AIR.**
They have **DESIRE** to be silent, cold drink.
>**OPEN AIR,** loosing clothing, perspiration, eating.
They have **DREAD/ FEAR** of **SUFFOCATION,** death, of heart disease, evil, ghosts or something bad will happen.

They have **CARDIAC** anguish, associated with **PALPITATION** and uneasiness in the region of heart. They have anxiety from **FEAR AND DYSPNEA.** They awaken in fright, as if from **SUFFOCATION.**

From mental exertion there arises prostration of mind. Past disagreeable events and thoughts torment them. They become discontented with everything, disgust with everything. Their mood becomes variable and repulsive.

< Thinking of complaints, excitement, dancing, uncovering.

They have **DREAMS** of weeping, scientific, mental and physical exertion,

Dream of fire *(means warning that you are **HEADING INTO DANGER** and need to be cautious)*,

murder, misfortune, full of cares, and

*Dream of **shooting** (means sense of underachieving)*

"GREAT DRYNESS OF MUCOUS MEMBRANE OF AIR PASSAGE."

CHAPTER TWENTY-ONE

SYPHILINUM

SYPHILINUM

RIGHT to LEFT SIDED (1+)

SYPHILIS (3+)

AFFECTED BY BOTH EXTREMES OF HEAT & COLD

As they have**FEAR** of **NIGHT** because their complaints < from sun down (darkness) to sunrise (day light).

They have FEAR of suffering from exhaustion on awakening. Fear of death. They especially have **FEAR OF PARALYSIS,** fear of catching cold.

They **DREAM**about **DISEASE, THEIR OWN DISEASE***(means NEGATIVITY, SORROW AND DESPAIR).*

Sad and lamenting, they don't want to be soothed, doubtful and despair of recovery (hopeless).They have sadness about disease.

Prostration of mind from mental exhaustion. Leads to difficulty in concentration while reading, studying, calculating. They become disobedience, anti social, striking himself, **KNOCKING** head against wall and things, Striking with fist.

They get offended easily, takes everything in bad part. **THEY WEEP AFTER ANGER,** sometimes they weep causelessly, laugh causelessly. They have indifference to loved ones, to relations, to future. They never speak truth *(liar)*. They themselves don't know what they are saying.

They dwell on past disagreeable occurrence. They have delusion/ mania/ impulse of **CLEANNESS, WASHING HAND.**

"EXTREME EMACIATION OF ENTIRE BODY."

Still they have egotism, self importance and delusion of grandeur.

They **DESIRE** to kill, they waste their money *(squander)*,alcohol.

They have **AVERSION** to business, meat.

< Consolation, sympathy, compassion, cold food.

>Daytime, cold bathing, changing of position.

"EXCESSIVE FLOW OF SALIVA, IT RUNS OUT OF MOUTH WHEN SLEEPING."

THUJA OCCIDENTALIS

THUJA OCCIDENTALIS

(TREE OF LIFE)
  (HOT & THIRSTY)
  LEFT SIDED (1+)
  RIGHT SIDED (1+)
  SYCOSIS (3+)
  SYPHILIS (2+)
  FAST PULSE (1+)
  SLOW PULSE (1+)

This is most famous and partially or superficially known remedy amount *LAY MEN* For <u>warts</u> but this remedy like any other remedy can be used for many things from *HEAD TO TOE*, depending upon symptom similarity.

They *HIDE TRUE FEELING.* They estranged from their family, especially wife ,from society. They are dishonest, disgust with everything. They get angry when things don't go after their will.

They *HAVE REJECTED FEELING* in themselves. They reproaches themselves. They are unreliable. They have disposition to become criminal or *ANTI- SOCIAL WITHOUT REMORSE.* They are full of *NARCISSIM,* self-esteem and egotism. They don't display their real character. They are manipulative , scheming and secretive.

They are irritable, jealous, quarrelsome, towards husband or mother, they control themselves among strangers and doctors. They have fake show of personality and altogether a different person at home.

They are hasty in walking, movement and occupation.

They have delusion of someone walks beside themselves.

Delusion he is pursued.

Delusion he is too thin, body is getting thin.

They have *WASHING/ CLEANESS MANIA, THEY ALWAYS WASHES THEIR HAND.*

They have **DREAM** *of* **ACCUSATION**(*means feeling of guilt*).

DREAMof *TEETH BREAKING OFF*(*means some kind of loss- relationship/ job*).

DREAM *of* **CATS**(*means malicious person nearby*).

DREAMof*FALLING FROM HIGH PLACE* (*means feeling out of control*).

They have **DREAMS** of murder, *of pollution which did not take place*, many, crowding one upon another, long, mental exertion, excelling in mental work, previous events, *DEATH-WHEN LYING ON LEFT SIDE,* dead bodies, *DANGER- WHEN LYING ON LEFT SIDE ,* calling out, *ANXIOUS-LYING ON LEFT SIDE,*

Dream of accident (*means crashing of hope*).

They have **FEAR** of stranger, touch, wind, of their own thought, that *JOINTS ARE WEAK,* disease, of others approaching him, apoplexy, with anxiety.

They have **DESIRE** to be silent, to weep all the time, walking, refreshing things, **tea, raw onion**, sour- fruit, open air, salty things, tobacco ,*FOR STOOL WHILE SMOKING.*

They have **AVERSION** to tobacco, potatoes, fresh meat, *TEA, ONION,* open air, to mental work, being touched, to company, presence of strangers.

<Yawning, wet weather, *FOGGY WEATHER,* standing, stretching out affected part, presence of stranger, walking, consolation, thinking of complaints, **onion, tea**, sugar, sweets, fish, coffee, *APPLE.*

>Occupied/ diverted, walking, *AFTER PERSPIRATION,* continued motion, lying on painless side, *FASTING,DISCHARGES*, descending, *CORYZA,* hot bathing, *FLATUS,ERUCTATION*, wine *YAWNING.*

" they are sensitive to onion and tea, having DESIRE, AVERSION OR AGGRAVATION from them."

"ANXIETY AFTER VACCINATION."

CHAPTER TWENTY-THREE

TUBERCULINUM

TUBERCULINUM

(HOT)

CORE words for tuberculinum remedy is **"RESIGNATION & FLYING".**

They have **DREAM** of flying *(means freedom),*

DREAM of being prude *(means tendency to be too out spoken).*

DREAM of shameful,

DREAM of journey means *(always have **desire** to start new everything).*

*Word **PRUDE** means people who are exaggerated proper, or excessively attentive to decorum.*

AFTER SEEING / LISTENING ABOUT OTHERS LIFE from social media and all. They also want to live life to the best level according to them. But in short span of time when they fail to achieve. This result in frustration. They become dissatisfied with children, with surrounding.

So they **DESIRE CHANGE***(places, symptoms, mood, job, partner)*, **DESIRE** to wander, to travel, to break things. Pull ones hair, want door and window open, cold air, ice-creams, smoked meat, refreshing things.

They have **AVERSION** to being touched, to mental work, **UNCOVERING,**

>Music, travel *(dromomania)*, cover, walking fast.

<Undressing, overeating, mental exertion, cold bathing, *coffee- smell.*

They have **DREAD/FEAR** of **ANIMALS***(CATS AND DOGS)*, of falling, of something bad will happen.

They torment themselves, throw things away and throw things at persons. Tear things , striking or knocking head against wall and things. They torture themselves; they have inclination to mutilate their body *(self torture).*They loss self control. They love to make people and animals suffer. They are destructive, vindictive, passionate, but rage followed by repentance, or quickly repents.

"THEY SAY THEY LOSE WEIGHT, DESPITE GOOD APPETITE."

CHAPTER TWENTY-FOUR

VERATRUM ALBUM

VERATRUM ALBUM

WHITE HELLEBORE
(HOT & THIRSTY)
RIGHT to LEFT SIDED (2+)
SLOW PULSE (2+)
FAST PULSE (2+)
They are **OUT OF TOUCH WITH REALITY.**

They **SWALLOW THEIR OWN FECES.** They do not recognize their relatives or anyone. They want to be naked *(shameless).* They estranged or ignore their relative, but kind with stranger. They are kind for superior and hard for inferior. They feel their **OWN IMPORTANCE.** They have delusion of wealth, hard work or **THEY ARE PRINCE** or a high rank person, so they become extravagance, waste and misuse or throw away their money. They keep on roving naked aimlessly, hilariously singing at night, whistles, talking excessively, especially on religious subjects.

They want to read religious books whole day with increased mental strength, they impulse to do strange things. During drunkenness they do striking. They wish to be considered **rich.**

They have delusion as if in heaven and talking to god or they are god or eating dirt or world is on fire.

They sit as if wrapped in deep sad thought & notices nothing never smiles with slowness of mind.

They have **AVERSION** to answer, to their own children, to husband, presence of others, company, thinking, touched, hot and warm food, **MELONS.**

They have **FEAR/DREAD** to **LOSE THE POSITION IN SOCIETY,** robbers, of being poisoned, diarrhoea, of being damaged, **OF DEATH *DURING MENSES,*** cholera, of being alone, of apoplexy during stool.

>**DISCHARGES, URINATION, PERSPIRATION, SECRETION** of mucus, uncovering, walking, mental exertion, occupied/ diverted, long after eating.

< During menses, talking others, company, **touching hairs,** interruption, climacteric period, fasting, farinaceous food, flatulent food, **grapes**, pan cakes, pastry, **pears**, pickles, raw food, sauerkraut, spoiled sausages, tea, veal, vegetables.

They have **DESIRES** to bite, to bite his shoe and swallowing the pieces, bite spoon, break thing, to be carried, carried fast, company, to escape, to go home, to leave home, wander, travel, **SPITTING IN FACES OF PEOPLE,** to be silent, **TO REMAIN IN BED FROM SEXUALEXCITEMENT,** cold food, sour fruit, **honey**, juicy things, lemon, milk, pickles, sardines.

They have **DREAMS** of water *(means emotions),*

Quarrel,

Robbers *(means feeling powerless),*

Being pursued by cats *(means malicious people nearby)*

Being pursued by dogs,

bitten by dogs *(**means betrayal**).*

Being pursued by animals, or animals pursuing him, anger and exhausting, frightful, **JUMPING, HUNTING,**

Accidents *(means crashing of hope).*

"COLD PERSPIRATION ON FOREHEAD *with all complaints."*

"COPIOUS EVACUATION-*VOMITING, STOOL, SALIVATION, SECRETION, DISCHARGES, SWEAT, URINE, WITH PROFOUND PROSTRATION."*

CHAPTER TWENTY-FIVE

ZINCUM METALLICUM

ZINCUM METALLICUM

(HOT & THIRSTY)
 RIGHT SIDED (2+)
 FAST PULSE (3+)
 SLOW PULSE (1+)

There is great greediness when eating, but they cannot eat fast enough *(SLOWNESS)*.

They repeat all questions before answering them. There is dullness of intellect *(SLOWNESS)*.

So there is **AVERSION** to **CONVERSATION**, to work, **MENTAL WORK**, being touched, solitude, noise, fish, warm food, bathing, meat, sugar, sweets, water.

They have **FEAR/DREAD** of chorea, work, superstitious, of robbers, of imaginary things, high places, of falling, death, dark, apoplexy. They get frightened easily, they **FEAR** of arrest on account/ believe of crime being committed.

They are sensitive to other's talking and noise.

< Climacteric period, darkness, **TALK OF OTHERS**, music, uncovering, walking fast, running ,sweets, sugar, spices, bathing, washing.

>Expectoration, eructation, fasting, diarrhoea, seminal emission, evening.

They have **DREAMS** of water(*means emotions*),

DREAM of **BEING STRANGLED**(*means you are feeling difficulty in expressing out*),

DREAM of STOOL(*reflection of freedom*),

soiling himself,

DREAM of BEINGSMEARED WITH STOOL(*means you are your own enemy*),

DREAMS of Robbers(*means feeling powerless*),

quarrels, being pursued,

DREAM of **DOGS CHANGING INTO HORSES**(*means lack of creativity ,power or strength*), murder, money,

DREAM of falling from high places(*means feeling out of control*),

knee pain, exhausting, goose, fleeing, fire, **MENTAL EXERTION, EXCREMENT,** soiling himself with excrement, **of ANIMALS,**

DREAM of ACCIDENTS(means crashing of hopes).

They have **DESIRE** for company, death, **TO PLAY DIRTY TRICK ON OTHERS,** to be fanned, cold food and cold drink.

They have **DELUSION** as if counting money or will be murdered or pursued by enemies/police.

They are full of cares, worries, about others and relatives.

They have **LACK OF CONFIDENCE.** There is prostration of mind from mental exhaustion. Their sense are dull, blunted, there is marked **slowness.**

There is **DIFFICULTY IN UNDERSTANDING.** They get easily offended, takes everything in bad part. They are despair about their recovery. They keep tormenting everyone with their complaints. They **WEEP WHEN**

ANGRY.

"IMPOTENT & POWERLESS MIND WITH FIDGETY OF FEET."

COUGH < SUGAR, SWEETMEATS.

CHAPTER TWENTY-SIX

HOT AND THIRSTLESS

APIS, allium cepa, *arg-n,* bry, calad, led, *lyc,* nat-m, op, **PULS,** thuja.

HOT AND THIRSTY

all-c, aloe, apis, ***ARG-N, BRY, fl-ac, IOD, kal-i, lach,*** lyc, ***NAT-M,*** nat-s, ***OP***, pic-ac, plat, puls, ***SECALE, SULPH, thuja.***

CHILLY AND THIRSTLESS

agn, am-c, ars, **bell, camph,** canth, caps, caust, chel, **CHINA,** cocc, **COLCH, con, cycl, ferr, HELL,** hep, ign, kal-ar, **kalic-carb,** mur-ac, nat-carb, nitric-ac, **NUX- M,** nux-v, oxal-ac, phos, **PH-AC, SABAD,** sars, **sepia,** spig, **staph, stram,** valer.

CHAPTER TWENTY-NINE

CHILLY AND THIRSTY

ACON, agar, agn, *ARS,* alum, aur, *bar-c, bell, CALC-C, camp, canth, carb-v, CAUST, CHAM, chel, CHIN,*cocc, colch, con,* cycl, *dulc,* graph, *HELL, hep, hyosc,* kali-ar, *kali-bi, kali-carb, kalm,* kreos, *mag-c, nat-c, nitric-ac,* nux-m, *nux-v,* ox-ac, *PHOS,* ph-ac, *plb, podo,* psor, *ran-b,* rhod, *RHUS-T,* ruta, sabad, sars, sepia, *SIL,* spig, staph, *STRAM,* stront, sul-ac, ther, *zinc.*

HOT REMEDIES

Aesc-h, all-c, aloe, ambra, *APIS, ARG-NIT, asf, aur-iod, aur m,* bar-iod, *bry, calad, calc-iod, calc-sulph, cocc-cati,* comoc, *crocus, dros,* fer-iod, *FLUOR-AC, grat, ham, IOD, KALI-IOD, KALI-SULPH, lach, led, lil-t, lyc, NAT-MUR, NAT-SUL,* niccol, *op,* picric-acid, *PLAT,* ptelia, *PULS, SABINA, SECALE, spong, sul, sul-iod,* thuj, tuber, ustil, *vespa,* viburn.

CHAPTER THIRTY-ONE

CHILLY REMEDIES

abrot, *acet-ac, acon, agar, agn, alumen, alum,Al-ph, alum-sil, am-c, apoc, arg-m,* ARS, ars-s-fl, asar, aur, aur-ars, aur-sulp,*bad, BAR-C, bar-m, bell,* benz-ac, *borax,* brom, *cadm, calc-ars, CALC-C, calc-fl, CALC-PH, calc-sil,* camph, *canth, CAPS, carb-an, carb-veg, carbn-sul,* card-m, *cauloph, CAUST, cham, chel, CHINA, chin-a, cimic, cistus, cocc, coff, colch, cycl, DULC, eupcon,hras, FERR, ferr-ars, form, GRAPH,* guaj, *hell, helon, HEP,* hyosc, *HYPER, ign, KALI-ARS, kali-bich, KALI-CARB, kali-chlor,* kali-phos, *kali-sil, kalm,kreos, lac-defl, MAGN-CARB, MAGN-PHOS, mang, MOSCH, mur-ac, nat-ars, natr-carb, NITRIC-ACID, nux-m, NUX-VOM, oxal-ax, petrol, PHOS, phos-ac, plb, pod,PSOR, PYROGEN, RAN-B,* rheum, *rhodo, RHUS, RUMEX, ruta, SABAD, sars, SEPIA, SIL, SPIG, stann,* staph, stram, **STRONT,***sul-ac, therid,* valer, viol-t, **zinc.**

CHAPTER THIRTY-TWO

THIRSTLESS REMEDIES

ANT-T, APIS, CHIN, COLCH, GELS, HELL, MENY, NUX-M, PH-AC, PULS, SABAD.

aesc, acon, am-m, ant-c, arg-n, ars, bell, bov, camph, con, cycl, dios, ferr, hydr-ac, ip, kali-c, lyc, mang, olnd, op, samb, sep, staph.

agar, aal-c, am-c, ambr, bry, bufo, calad, canth, caps, caust, chel, cimic, cocc, cor-r, crot-t, hep, ign, iris, kali-p, led, merc-c, mez, mur-ac, nat-c, nat-m, nat-s, nit-ac, nux-v, ox-ac, petr, phos, plat, sars, spig, stram, sulph, tab, thuj, valer, verat.

CHAPTER THIRTY-THREE

THIRSTY REMEDIES

ACON, ARG-N, ARS, BRY, CALC, CALC-S, CAPS, CAUST, CHAM, CHIN, DIG, EUP-PER, HELL, IOD, MERC, NAT-M, OP, PHOS, RHUS-T, SEC, SIL, STRAM, SULPH, TARENT, VERAT.

all-c, am-m, anac, ant-c, apoc, arn, ars-i, bapt, bar-c, bar-m, bell, berb, bol, bor, calc-ar, camph, canth, carb-ac, carb-v, chel, chin-a, chin-s, cic, cimic, cina, coc-c, cocc, colch, coloc, con, croc, crot-c, crot-h, cupr, dros, culc, ferr-p, fl-ac, hep, hyos, kali-bi, kali-c, kali-i, kali-p, kali-s, kal,m, lach, laur, led, mag-c, merc-c, merc-i-f, mez, nat-a, nat-c, nat-p, nit-ac, nux-v, plb, podo, ran-b, raph, rat ther, thuj, verat-v, zinc.

aesc, aeth, agar, agn, all-s, aloe, alum, am-c, ant-t, apis, aur, cor-r, glon, graph, ip, kreos, lil-t, lyc, mag-m, mag-s, mur-ac, naja, nat-s, nux-m, ox-ac, petr, ph-ac, pic-ac, plat, psor, puls, rhod, rob, ruta, sabad,samb, sang, sars, sel, sep, spig, stann, staph, stront, sul-ac, tab.

CHAPTER THIRTY-FOUR

WARM FOOT

CHAM, PULS, SUPH.

apis, arund, caust, cocc, glon, kali-bi, lyc, nat-s, nux-v, petr, psor, ruta, sec, sep, sil.

acon, agar, ang, arn, ars-h, ars, aster, brom, bufo, calad, calc, camp, carb-an, carb-s, carb-v, cimic, coff, coloc, crot-h, cub, hyos, ign, kali-ar, kali-chl, kali-i, lach, laur, led, merc, mez, mill, morph, nat-c, nat-m, nat-p, nit-ac, par, ph-ac, phos, phy, ptel, rhem, rhus-t, rhus-v, spig, spong, stann, staph, sumb, til, vip, zinc.

CHAPTER THIRTY-FIVE

WARM SOLE

LYC, SULPH.

calc, carl, cham,cocc, ferr, graph, lach, lil-t, manc, nat-c, nux-v, petr, ph-ac, phos, puls, sang, sanic, sep, sil.

am-m, apoc, ars-s-f, bell, berb, carb-s, carb-v, clem, coc-c, cub, dulc, eup-per, ferr-p, fl-ac, kali-n, lith, mang, med, mur-ac, nat-m, nit-ac, nux-m, ox-ac, plb, psor, samb, sars, spig, stann, stram, verat, zinc.

CONCLUSION

In these **25 remedies** . I have mentioned *various* **DREAMS** ...like

DREAMS of-accidents,
Being pursued by wild animals or horses,
Journey by water full of snakes,
Drowning,
Falling,
Funerals,
Marriages,
Danger,
Snakes,
Being bitten by snakes,
Fishes,
Insects,
Putrid water,
Dead friends,
Ghost,
Hunger,
Danger from water,
Dead bodies,
Black water,
Cats,
Difficulties,
Unsuccessful,
Sick people,
Disease,
Bitten by dogs,
Murder,
Fire,

Meeting friends,
Robbers,
Journey,
Water,
Sea,
Injuries,
Being stabbed,
Dispute for money,
Dead relatives,
Mental exertion,
Being buried alive,
Falling into water,
Of being murdered,
Of being beaten,
Of children being beaten,
Quarrel with dead relatives,
Suffocation,
Calling out for help,
Riots,
Of stabbing others,
Full of inventions,
Death of friend,
Being accused of theft,
Urinating,
Swimming,
Boat,
Boat foundering,
Disease-pain,
Fight,
Flying,
Flood,
Difficulties with journey,
Falling from height,

Shooting,
Rebellion,
Firearms,
Swallowing pins,
Being bitten by animals(dogs),
Being taken as a prisoner,
Accusation,
Crime,
Teeth pulled out,
Being to die,
Someone is lying under him,
Being pursued by dogs & cats,
Cruelty,
Falling out teeth,
Worms,
Exhaustion,
Lascivious,
Amorous,
Blood,
Haemorrhages,
Defecation in open,
Black dogs,
Black animals,
Ghosts,
Naked men,
Gold ,
Money,
Rowing,
Running,
Ascending,
Climbing,
Falling from downstairs,
Business of the day,

Body or face disfigured,
Fight with ghost,
Going & lost in forest,
Rat , mice,
Rape,
Being pursued must run backward,
Being burn,
Someone is calling,
Of youth time,
Past events,
Storm,
Being pursued by ghost,
Battle,
Having been betrayed,
Shameful,
Other seeing him naked while bathing or defecating,
Adventurous,
Fire coming down from the heaven,
Being crushed,
Danger of death,
BEING SHOT,
GYMNASTICS,
BEING PURSUED BY GIANTS,
SHOOTING,
GIANTS,
VERMIN,
BATTLE,
WALKING.
SWIMMING IN WATER,
RUNNING,
RIDING IN A CARRIAGE,
ASSASSINS,
HOUSEHOLD,

BEING BUSY,
HIGH WAVES,
CLIFF,
FALLING INTO WELL,
SEA STORM,
DEEP WELL,
RAPID TRANSIT FROM PLACE TO PLACE,
NIGHTMARES,
WOUND,
FEASTING,
SOLEMNITIES,
MISFORTUNE,
BEING WOUNDED,
SOMEONE CALLING OUT,
OLD SCHOOLMATE,
OLD FRIENDS,
HOT STOVE,
JUMPING GREAT LEAPS,
BEING A GIRL,
DIRTY ROADS,
WALKING ON DIRTY ROADS,
WALKING OVER HOT FLOOR,
DOGS,
ROMANTIC,
HORSES,
SHAMEFUL,
SORE THROAT,
ADVENTURE,
WADING IN WATER,
PREACHING,
PURSUED BY ENEMIES,
DEAD FRIEND,
DEATH OF FRIEND,

PUSUED BY SOLDIERS,
WILD ANIMALS,
BATTLES,
HISTORIC,
HEARING GUNSHOT,
SHOOTING,
CROCODILE,
REMORSE,
BEING PURSUED BY WILD ANIMALS,
PAIN,
DRINKING,
EXHAUSTING,
TEETH BREAKING OFF,
ACCUSATION,
POLLUTION WHICH DIDN'T TAKE PLACE,
DANGER OR DEATH OR ANXIOUS WHEN LYING
ON LEFT SIDE,
WALKING IN MUD,
WADING IN MUD,
SOILING HIMSELF,
WALKING IN EXCREMENT,
DAUGHTER FALLING INTO WATER,
MUD,
SOILING HIMSELF WITH EXCREMENT,
UNSUCCESSFUL IN COITION,
DRAGONS,
SKELETON,
BEING SATBBED,
STOOL,
BEING CLOSET,
EXELLING IN MENTAL WORK,
OF HELP,
DON'T SUCCEED IN BUSINESS,

WEEPING,

SCIENTIFIC,

DISEASE,

THEIR ON DISEASE,

BEING PRUD,

JUMPING,

HUNTING,

BEING STRANGLED,

BEING SMEARED WITH STOOL,

DOGS CHANGING INTO HORSES,

MONEY,

STOOL,

According to my experience **DREAMS** let you know *the innermost personality of the person*.

DREAM is a specific expression .They reveals a lot. They begins mostly in the evening, a time when threshold of consciousness is lowered & impulses & images of the unconscious can pass across it.

Function of the dream is to restore our *psychological balance/equilibrium*.

Sometimes what we fail to see/observe during **CASE TAKING** these **DREAMS** pass on the key information to us. After knowing little bit about dream analysis *we can cross question* our PATIENTS/CLIENTS.

Although we know it is plain *foolishness to completely believe* in readymade systematic guides to dream interpretation , as interpretation can vary from person to person according to "Carl jung".

& **HOMOEOPATHY** is all about *Individualization*.

Finally I will say don't make any *fixed ideas* regarding anything. Always keep your focus on *unbiased*CASE TAKING (Never try to skip this).

Good luck..

Dr sandeep sairal

9 798886 412277